GUINEA PIGS

MICHAELA MILLER

Contents

Heinemann Interactive Library
Des Plaines, Illinois

Wild Ones

Wild guinea pigs are called cavies and most of them live in Peru. They like to spend their days eating grass, leaves, and plant stems. They sleep and shelter under logs, in caves, and in **burrows**.

wild guinea pigs

Wild guinea pigs like to live in big family groups.

3

The Guinea Pig for You

There are many kinds of guinea pigs. They have different colored fur and different fur lengths. Some, like the Peruvian guinea pig, are long-haired.

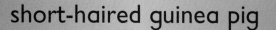

short-haired guinea pig

GUINEA PIG FACT

Guinea pigs can live for up to seven years.

Long-haired guinea pigs are quite difficult to look after. Their coats need a lot of brushing to keep them untangled. Short-haired guinea pigs are best for first-time owners.

Where to Find Your Guinea Pig

Animal shelters are often looking for good homes for guinea pigs. You can also buy your guinea pigs from **breeders**. A good breeder will let you ask lots of questions. They will check their guinea pigs are going to good homes.

A veterinarian could tell you about local breeders and animal shelters. Do not buy your guinea pig from anywhere that looks dirty.

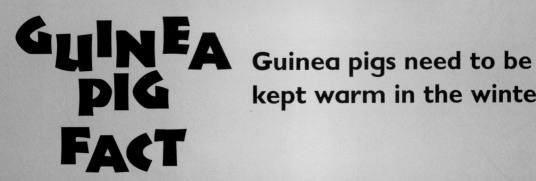

GUINEA PIG FACT

Guinea pigs need to be kept warm in the winter.

A Healthy Guinea Pig

Choose two male guinea pigs or two females from the same **litter**. They should be between six and eleven weeks old. They should have smooth coats and clean ears, eyes, mouths, noses, and tails. Healthy guinea pigs run around their home quite happily.

young guinea pigs eating lettuce

GUINEA PIG FACT

If you put two male or two female adult guinea pigs together who don't know each other, they may fight.

Do not choose a guinea pig that seems to have no energy and is crouching in a corner. It is probably not very healthy.

Safe Hands

Move toward your guinea pig from the front, rather than from the side. This does not frighten it so much. Pick it up very gently with one hand under its bottom and the other around its shoulders.

Do not let it wriggle or jump from your arms because it could really hurt itself.

Your guinea pigs will probably like being brushed gently with a baby's hairbrush every day.

GUINEA PIG FACT

Guinea pigs can be very timid and can get upset if you hold them a lot before they are used to it.

Feeding Time

Guinea pigs need lots of water. Attach a drip-fed water bottle with a metal spout to the side of your guinea pigs' house and exercise area, and make sure it is always full.

GUINEA PIG FACT

Guinea pigs need lots of vitamin C, which they get from green leaves and vegetables.

You can buy special guinea pig food from pet supply stores. Feed each guinea pig about two to three ounces every day plus some raw fruit and vegetables. Put the food in heavy bowls.

Home Sweet Home

Get the biggest cage you can for your guinea pigs. For two guinea pigs it should be at least 4 feet by 2 feet by $1\frac{3}{4}$ feet. It should have a sleeping area with a solid door and a living area with a wire mesh front. You should also give them a **run** in the yard when the weather is good.

cage

run

The cage should be high off the ground. If you keep the cage outside, it should be moved inside into a warm garage, or the house in cold weather.

an indoor exercise area

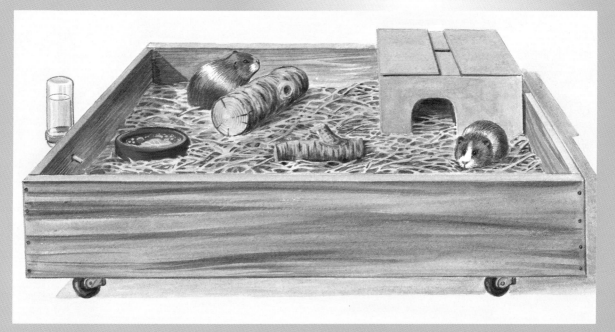

15

Keeping Clean

The guinea pigs' cage should be cleaned often to keep your pets healthy. Wet patches and droppings should always be removed.

The cage will need to be thoroughly cleaned at least four times a year.

Guinea pigs need deep, soft bedding like hay and straw to sleep and **burrow** in. Under this, and throughout the whole cage, there should be a two-inch-deep layer of sawdust, cat litter, or wood chips.

At the Veterinarian

Take your guinea pigs to the veterinarian once a year for a checkup. The veterinarian will look out for things like overlong teeth and claws.

Watch your guinea pigs every day very carefully for signs of illness. Always check their teeth, eyes, nose, and bottom. If they do not want to eat, seem tired, or even seem to have a cold, take them to the veterinarian immediately.

GUINEA PIG FACT

A hardwood **gnawing block** will give your guinea pig something to gnaw on and stop its teeth getting too long.

No More Babies

It really is not a good idea to let your guinea pigs have babies. Female guinea pigs (sows) can have five **litters** a year and four babies in each litter.

GUINEA PIG FACT

If rabbits and guinea pigs meet when they are very young, they can live together. Each should have its own private space in their cage.

Finding homes for baby guinea pigs can be a real problem. It is very difficult to get guinea pigs **neutered** so they do not have babies. So only keep guinea pigs of the same sex together.

A Note From the ASPCA

Pets are often our good friends for the very best of reasons. They don't care how we look, how we dress, or who our friends are. They like us because we are nice to them and take care of them. That's what being friends is all about.

This book has given you information to help you know what your pet needs. Learn all you can from this book and others, and from people who know about animals, such as veterinarians and workers at animal shelters like the ASPCA. You will soon become your pet's most important friend.

More Books to Read

Chrystie, Frances N. *Pets: A Comprehensive Handbook for Kids.* **New York: Little, 1994.**

King–Smith, Dick. *I Love Guinea Pigs.* **London: Candlewick Press, 1995.**

Glossary

When words in this book are in bold, **like this,** they are explained in this glossary.

animal shelters   There are lots of these shelters all around the country that look after unwanted pets and try to find them new homes.

breeders   These are people who let their guinea pigs have babies. They then sell the babies.

burrows   These are underground holes and tunnels.

gnawing block   This is a special bark-covered log of wood for guinea pigs to chew on. It stops their teeth from getting too long.

litter   A group of new born guinea pigs born to one mother is called a litter.

neutered   This is an operation to stop an animal being able to have babies.

run   An outdoor area where the guinea pigs can run free when the weather is good is called a run. It should be fenced on all sides with a mesh cover on the top. This keeps the guinea pigs safe from cats, dogs, and birds.

23

Index

Published by Heinemann Interactive Library, an imprint of Reed Educational & Professional Publishing,
1350 East Touhy Avenue, Suite 240 West, Des Plaines, IL 60018
© 1998 RSPCA

Produced by Times Offset (M) Sdn. Bhd.
Designed by Nicki Wise and Lisa Nutt
Illustrations by Michael Strand

02 01 00 99 98
10 9 8 7 6 5 4 3 2 1

Library of Congress Cataloging-in-Publication Data
Miller, Michaela, 1961-
  Guinea pigs / Michaela Miller.
  p. cm. — (Pets)
  Includes bibliographical reference and index.
  Summary: A simple introduction to choosing and caring for guinea pigs.
  ISBN 1-57572-575-4 (lib. bdg.)
  1. Guinea pigs as pets — Juvenile literature. [1. Guinea pigs.
2. Pets.] 1. Title. II. Series: Miller, Michaela. 1961- Pets.
SF459.G9M54 1998   97-11985
636.9'3592—dc21   CIP
                                  AC

Acknowledgements
The author and publishers are grateful to the following for permission to reproduce copyright photographs.
Dave Bradford pp4, 5, 7, 10-13, 20, 21; Bruce Coleman Ltd/ p2 Gunter Zeisler; NHPA/ p3 E A Janes; RSPCA/ p6 Colin Seddon , p8 Angela Hampton, p9 Judyth Platt, pp18, 19 Tim Sambrook.
Cover photographs reproduced with permission of : RSPCA
With special thanks to the ASPCA and their consultant Dr. Stephen Zawistowski, who approved the contents of this book.
Every effort has been made to contact copyright holders of any material reproduced in this book.
Any omissions will be rectified in subsequent printings if notice is given to the publisher.